JAZZ FOR THE RECORDER

A CONTRASTING SELECTION OF POPULAR JAZZ STANDARDS, TOGETHER WITH A TWO PAGE INTRODUCTION TO PLAYING THE RECORDER

Selected and arranged for Recorder by Peter J Lavende

Wise Publications
London/New York/Sydney/Cologne

Exclusive Distributors:

Music Sales Limited
78 Newman Street, London W1P 3LA, England

Music Sales Corporation
799 Broadway, New York, N.Y., 10003, USA

Music Sales Pty. Limited
27 Clarendon Street, Artarmon, Sydney, NSW 2064, Australia

Music Sales GmbH
Kolner Strasse 199, 5000 Cologne 90, West Germany

ISBN 0 86001 919-5

Order No. AM 28994

Originated and printed in England by
Halstan & Co. Ltd., Amersham, Bucks.

Contents

Playing and Care of the Recorder

HOLDING THE RECORDER

The recorder has eight holes, seven on the front and one in the rear. It is held with the left hand on the top portion and the right hand on the lower. The left thumb covers the rear hole and the other fingers follow as shown in the accompanying diagram.

Each finger covers only the hole assigned to it, and no other. This never varies. The right thumb is used only to support the instrument and the left little finger is not used at all.

FINGERING DIAGRAM

LEFT HAND

Left thumb hole O — O 1st finger

O 2nd finger

O 3rd finger

RIGHT HAND

O 1st finger

O 2nd finger

O 3rd finger

O 4th finger

When hole is:

O = do not finger

● = close completely

◐ = open

◒ = left thumbhole pinched (approximately 7/10 closed)

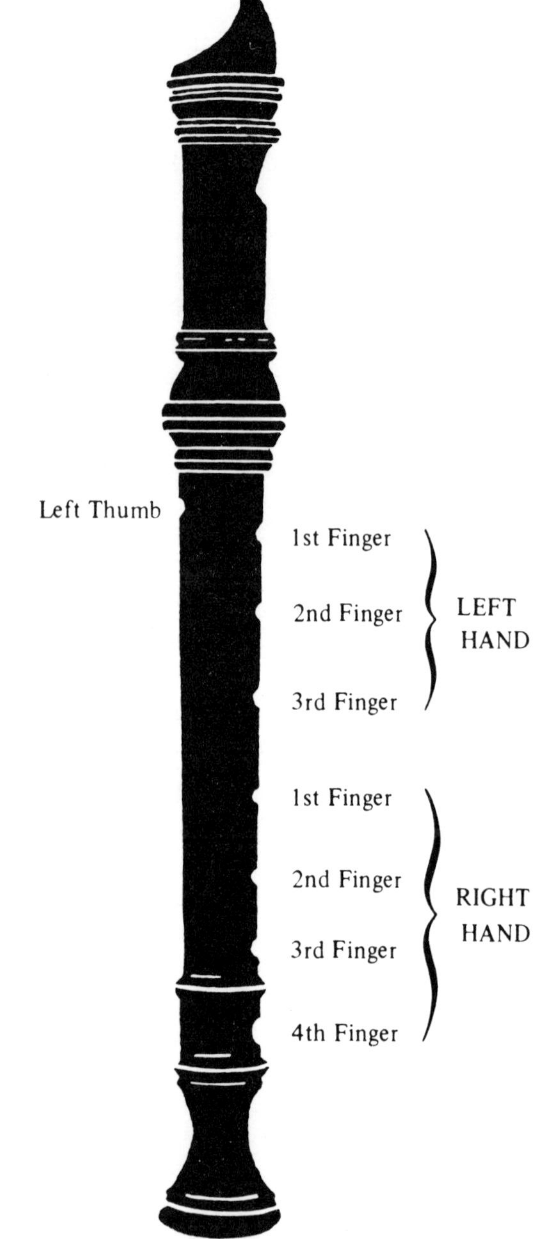

FINGERING

Fingering the recorder should be done firmly, yet not with heavy pressure. When a hole is to be covered, it must be covered completely. The finger tips are not used, but rather the soft pads of the fingers. Fingers not in use should be kept about one half inch above the holes to which they are assigned, and when called into play should fall like little hammers and with gentle force.

The recorder is supported by the lips and right thumb. The right thumb is positioned approximately behind the first finger of the right hand. The recorder is held to the lips at a 45 degree angle. The elbows are held away from the body, slightly forward and up.

BREATHING

Blowing through the recorder must be done with an even and constant breath pressure. This is so important that you would do well to re-read and commit this to memory.

Should you increase the breath pressure while playing, the tone will become higher (sharp) and if diminished, the tone will become lower (flat). The result will be an out of tune performance.

The proper pressure to produce a good tone will vary. In general, the lower tones require less pressure than the middle range, while the higher tones need a stronger pressure. However, whatever pressure used, it must be kept constant for the duration of the note.

TONGUING

Tonguing is a device for starting and stopping a tone and giving the sound definition. It is one of the most important recorder techniques to understand and develop correctly from the start.

The recorder mouthpiece is placed between the lips with a slight grip. The teeth and tongue never touch the instrument. Let your tongue find the ridge in your upper mouth about where the teeth go into the gums. With the recorder between the lips and tongue in position, softly say the syllable "DAH". Do this several times in succession, and the last time say "DAH - d". Do this until it becomes automatic.

What you have done would look like this:

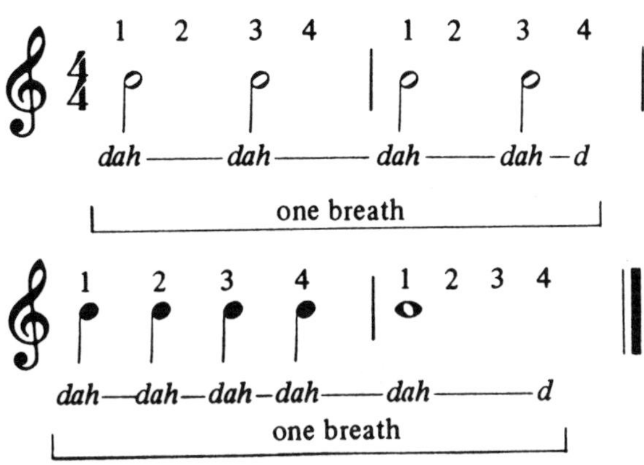

STACCATO has the effect of shortening the duration of a note. The shortness of the note will depend upon the character of the piece.

Staccato notes are indicated by dots over the notes. Tonguing is slightly different for staccato and looks like this:

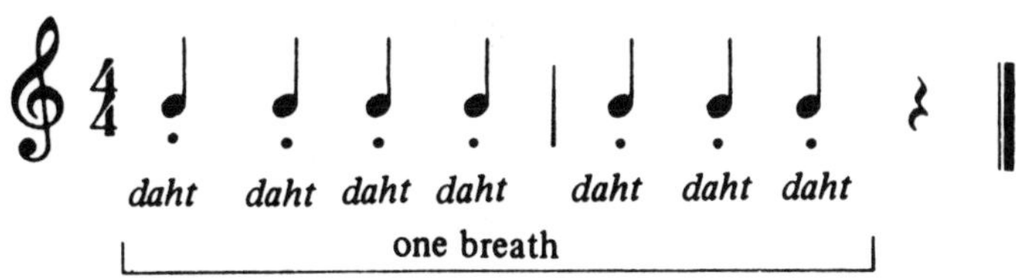

LEGATO is indicated by a curved line connecting two or more different tones. The first note in the slur is tongued with DAH - the AH sound is maintained for the other notes within the slur, and the last note in the slur is ended with the final 'd' sound. It looks like this:

Where there are other notes following and not included in the slur, and no breath marks or rest occur, the final 'd' is omitted from the slur until called for:

CARE OF THE RECORDER

Before playing your recorder, warm the mouthpiece in your hand. This will help hold moisture condensation in the windway to a minimum.

Most recorders are furnished with a swab. If yours is not, use a soft piece of cloth on a stick and wipe out the instrument after each playing. Be careful not to touch the delicate lip in the window. Damage to the lip will alter the tone.

When assembling the parts use a slow twisting motion to avoid forcing and damaging the joints.

If the joints become loose, wrap them with transparent tape. If they become tight, rub them with a light grease.

If moisture collects in the windway while playing, hold your finger over the slot and blow the moisture out.

Wooden recorders should be treated with the care given any delicate piece of wood. They should not be exposed to extremes of heat or cold.

Read and follow the direction sheet enclosed with most recorders.

TUNING THE RECORDER

Instruments may vary slightly in pitch. For group playing, close tuning is desired. Have each person sound B. Listen carefully for the lowest sounding B. Then each recorder may be lowered in pitch by twisting it apart at the top (tuning) joint, thereby lengthening the instrument. Shorten and lengthen each recorder by small adjustments until all are tuned to the lowest B.

Recorder Fingering Chart

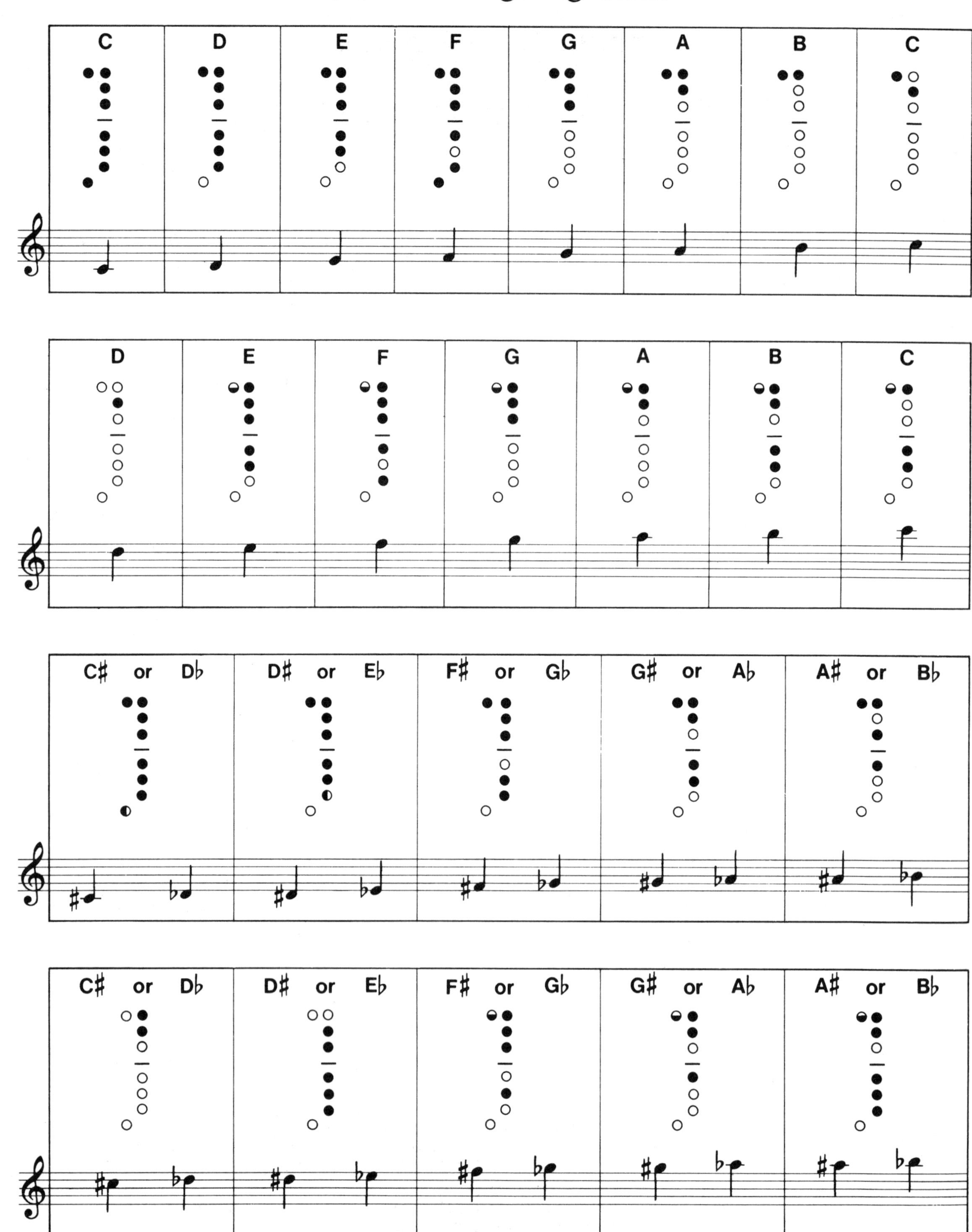

Basin Street Blues

CHORDS USED IN THIS SONG:

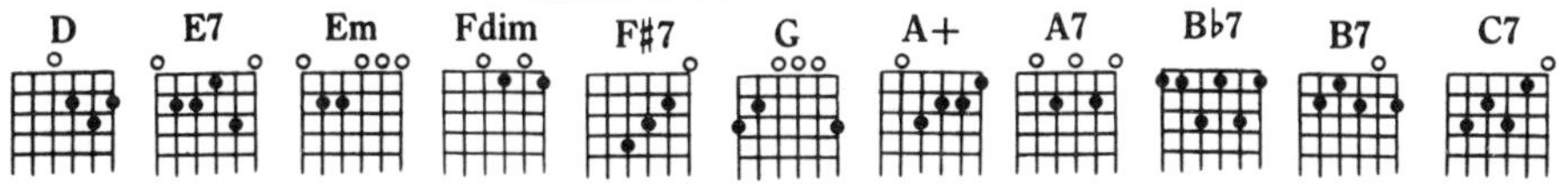

D E7 Em Fdim F♯7 G A+ A7 B♭7 B7 C7

Words and Music by
SPENCER WILLIAMS

Moderato

Won't cha come a-long with me_ To the Mis - sis - sip-pi?__

We'll take the boat_ to the land of dreams,_ Steam down the riv - er down to New Or - leans._ The

band's there to meet us,__ old friends to greet us,__

Where all the black and the white folks meet,_ This is Ba-sin Street._

Ba - sin Street_ is the street,_ where dark e - lite.__ Al - ways meet_ in

New Or - leans,_ land of dreams, You'll nev - er know how nice it seems or just how much it real - ly means.

Glad to be__ yes sir - ee,__ where wel-come's free,__ dear to me,__ where

I can lose,_ My Ba - sin Street Blues.__

rall.

Tuxedo Junction

CHORDS USED IN THIS SONG:

Words by
BUDDY FEYNE

Music by
ERSKINE HAWKINS, WILLIAM JOHNSON & JULIAN DASH

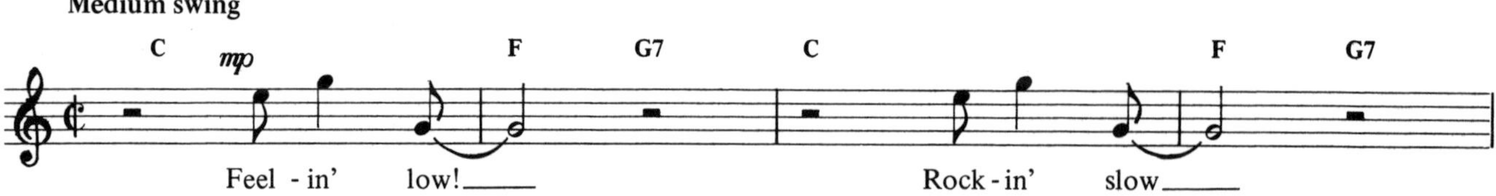

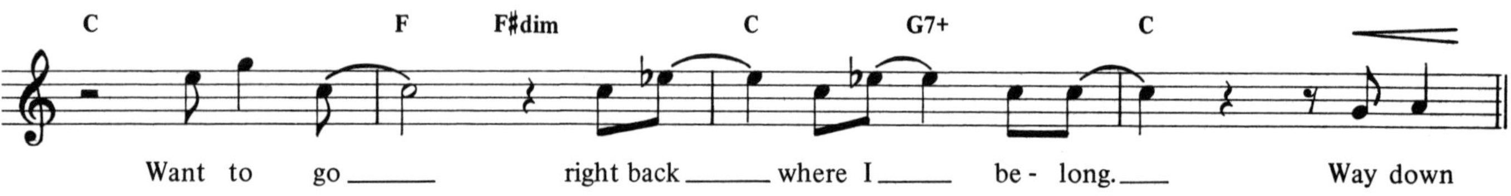

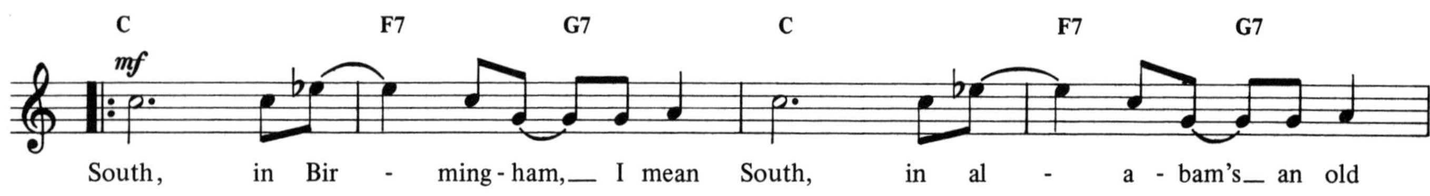

C F7 F♯dim C G7 C C7
jive, That makes you want to dance 'til break of day. It's a

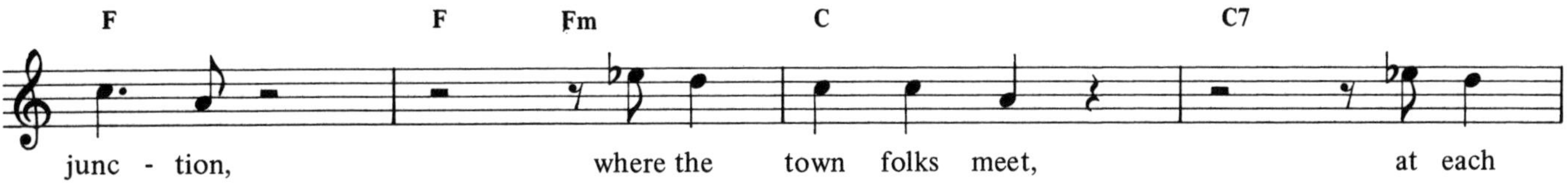
F F Fm C C7
junc - tion, where the town folks meet, at each

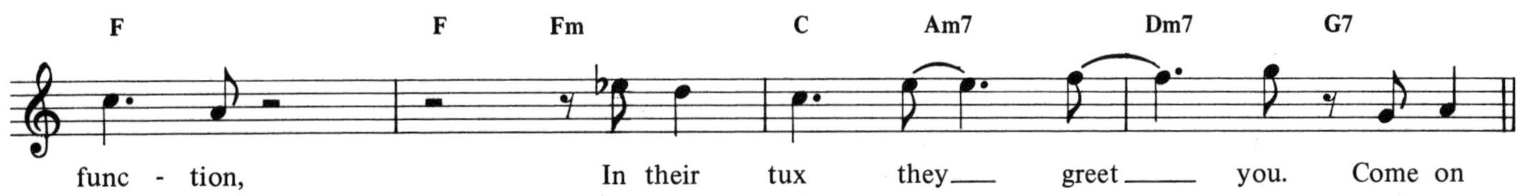
F F Fm C Am7 Dm7 G7
func - tion, In their tux they greet you. Come on

C F G7 C F G7
down, For - get your care come on down, You'll find me me there, so long

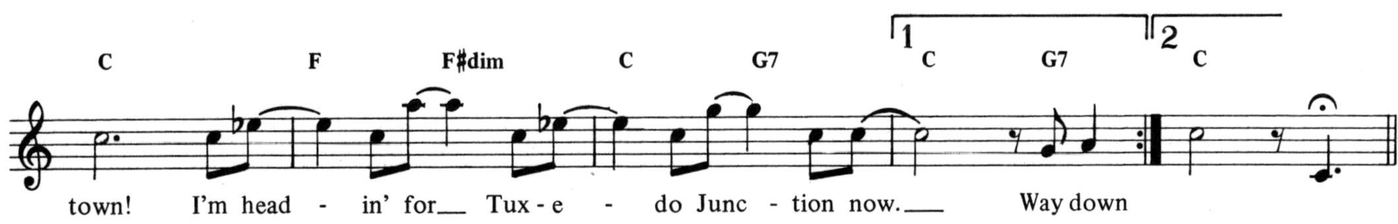
1 2
C F F♯dim C G7 C G7 C
town! I'm head - in' for Tux - e - do Junc - tion now. Way down

Bugle Call Rag

CHORDS USED IN THIS SONG:

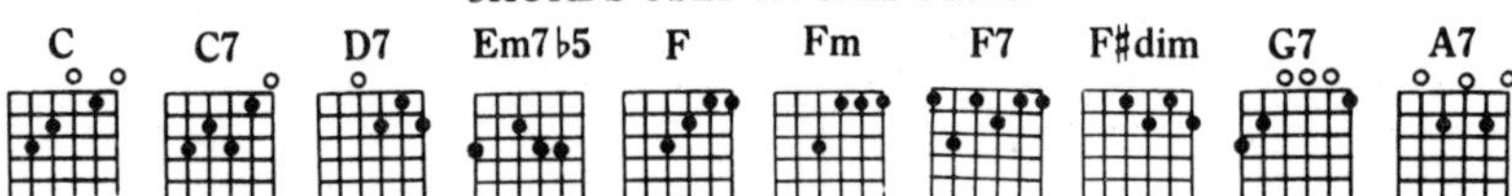

Words and Music by
JACK PETTIS, BILLY MEYERS & ELMER SCHOEBEL

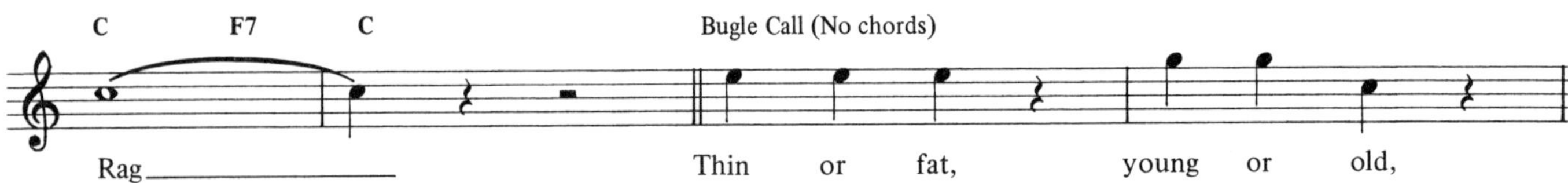

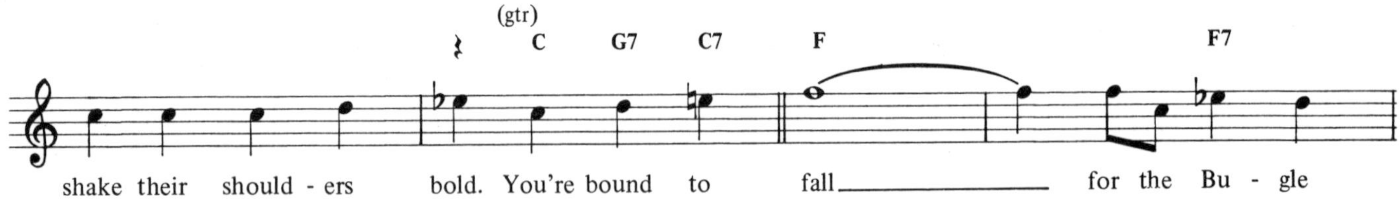

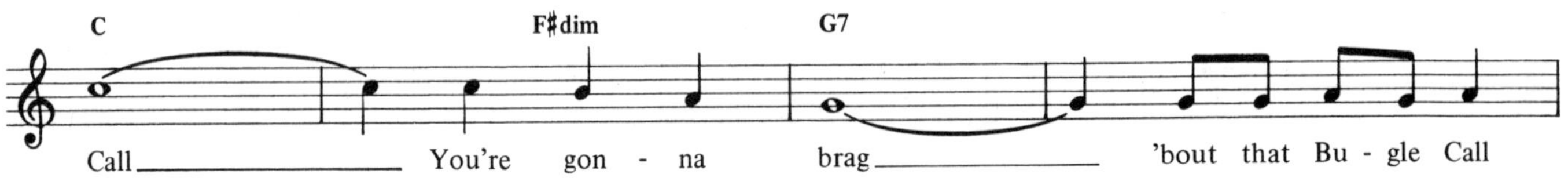

C
C7
F7
Rag
Hold me ba - by let's syn - co - pate

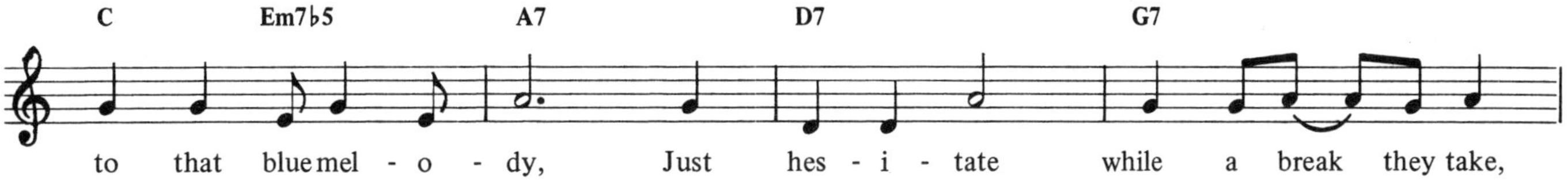
C
Em7♭5
A7
D7
G7
to that blue mel - o - dy, Just hes - i - tate while a break they take,

C
F7
While we're dan - cing please hold me tight,

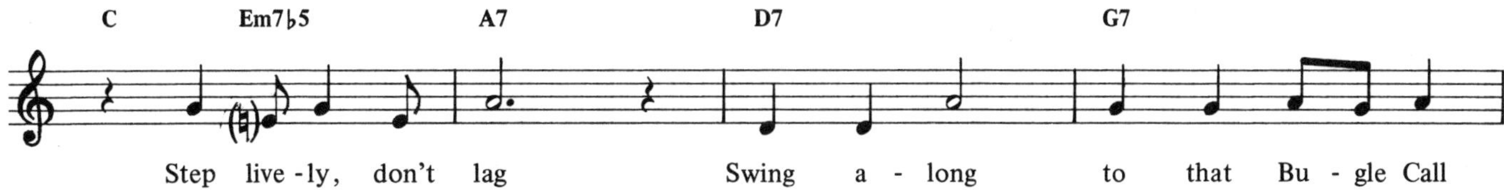
C
Em7♭5
A7
D7
G7
Step live - ly, don't lag Swing a - long to that Bu - gle Call

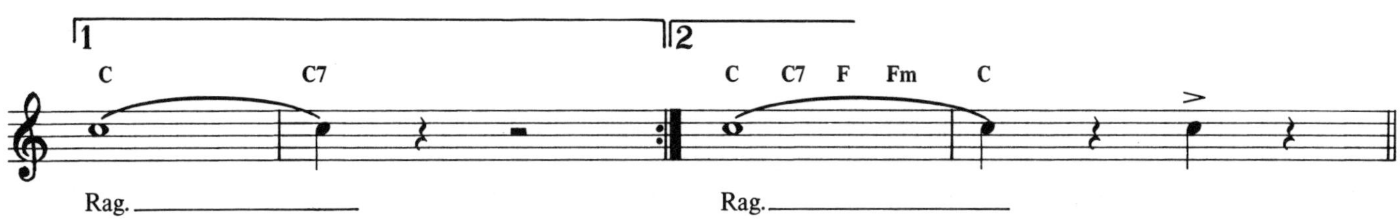
1
2
C
C7
C C7 F Fm C
Rag.
Rag.

Midnight In Moscow

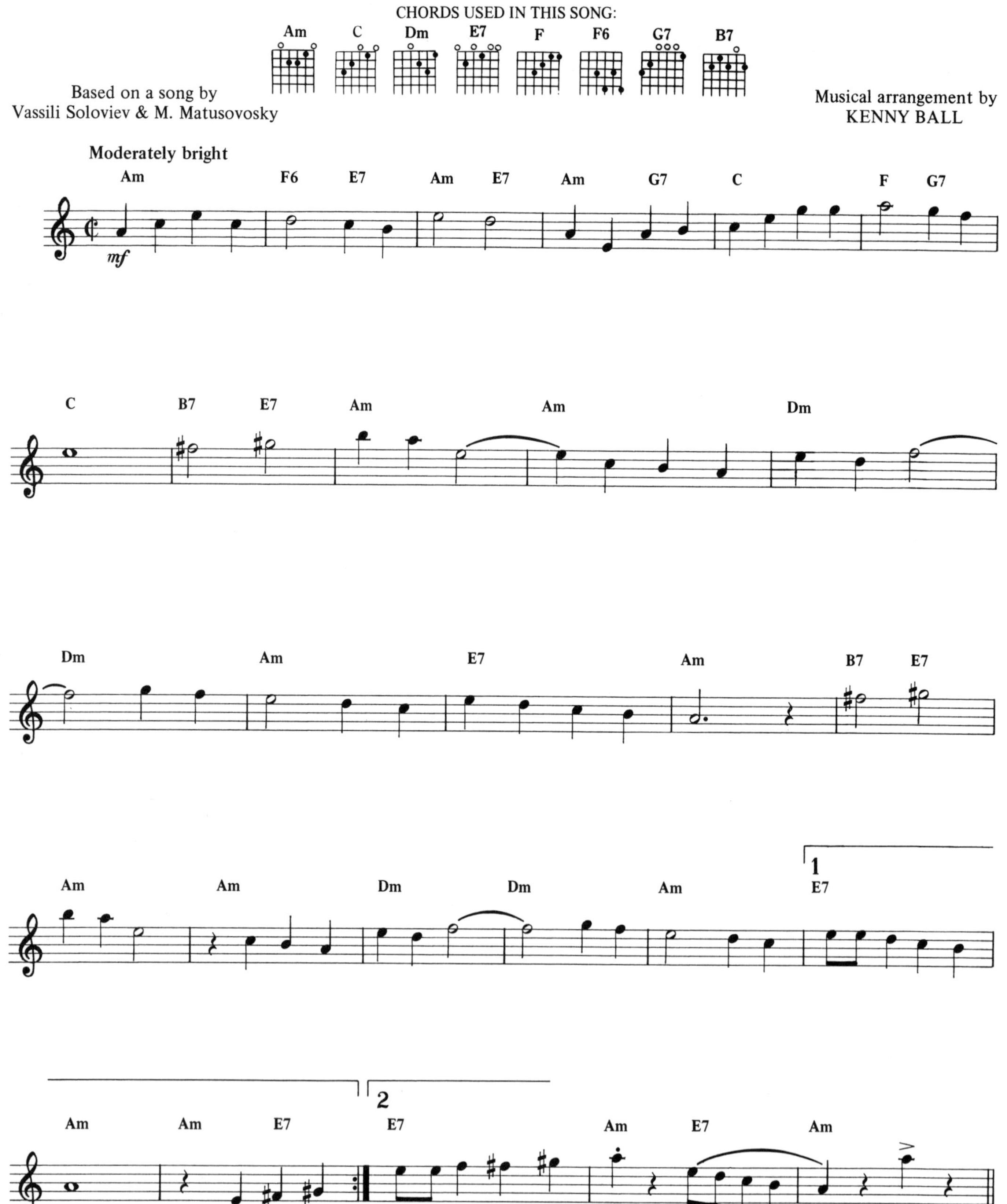

Mood Indigo

CHORDS USED IN THIS SONG:
G G7 A7 A9 Am B♭dim C C7 Dm
D+ D7 E♭7 E♭dim Edim Em F7
Words and Music by
DUKE ELLINGTON, IRVING MILLS & ALBANY BIGARD
Very slow, with expression
mp
You ain't been blue No, No, No, You ain't been blue
Till you've had that mood in - di- go, That feel - in'
goes steal - in' down to my shoes, While I sit and sigh,
"Go 'long, blues." Al - ways get that
mf
mood in - di - go, Since my ba - by said good - bye. In the eve - nin'
when lights are low, I'm so lone-some I could cry 'Cause there's no-bo-dy who
cares a-bout me, I'm just a soul who's blu - er than blue can be. When I get that
mood in - di - go I could lay me down and die. die.

African Waltz

CHORDS USED IN THIS COMPOSITION:

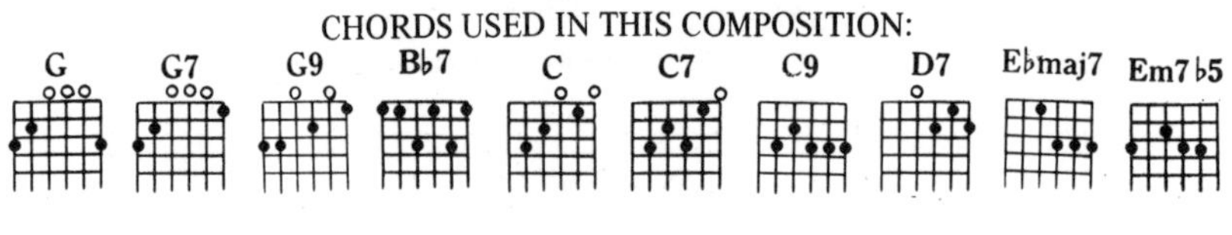

by
GALT MacDERMONT

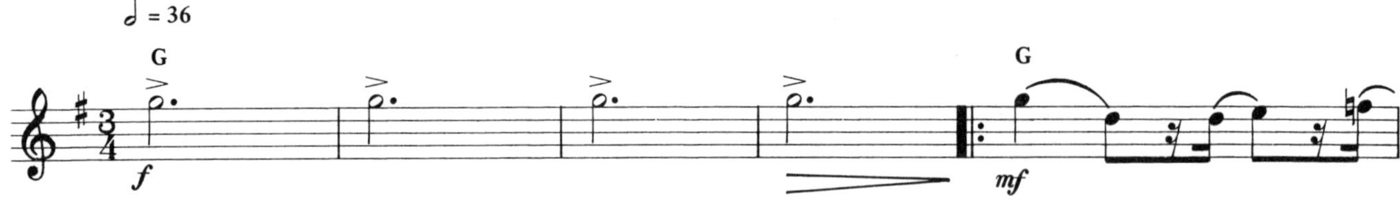

G7
C7

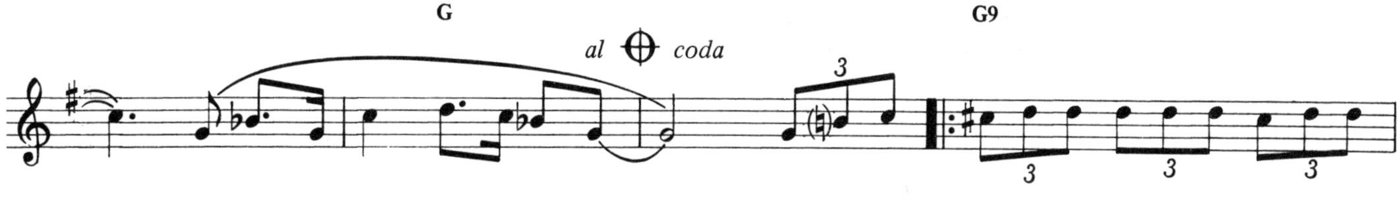
G
al coda
G9

C9

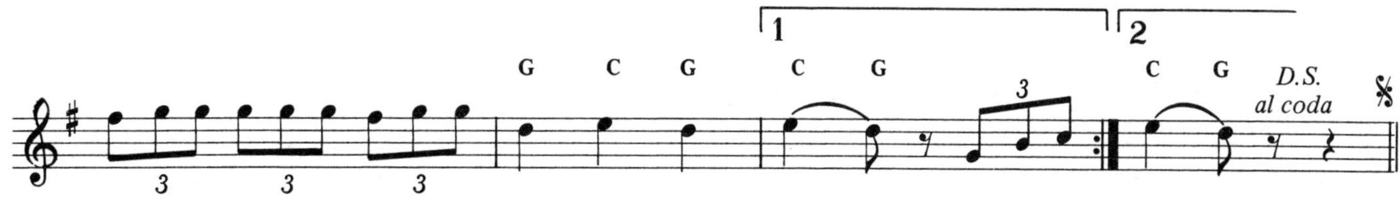
1
2
G C G
C G
C G
D.S.
al coda

CODA
G
f

Boogie Woogie Bugle Boy

CHORDS USED IN THIS SONG:

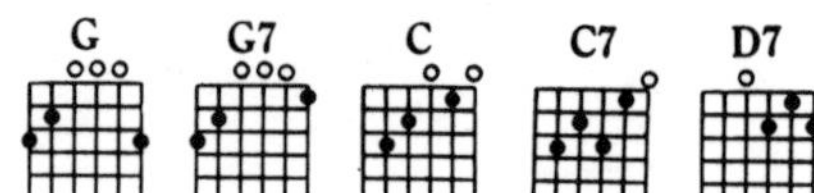

Words and Music by
DON RAYE & HUGHIE PRINCE

Medium Boogie Woogie

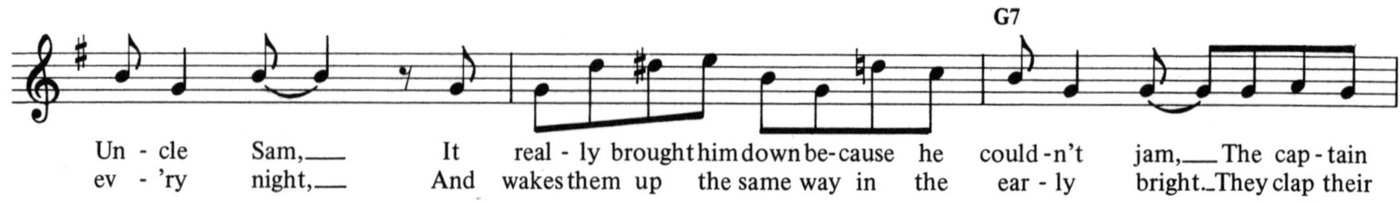

C
G
seemed to un-der - stand ___ Be-cause the next day the "cap" ___ went out and
hands and stamp their feet ___ Be-cause they know how he plays ___ when some-one
D7
C7
draft-ed a band, ___ And now the comp-'ny jumps ___ when he plays re - veil - le, He's the
gives him a beat, ___ He real - ly breaks it up ___ when he plays re - veil - le, He's the
G
Boo - gie Woo - gie Bu - gle Boy of Com - pa - ny B. A toot! A toot! A
toot did-dle ah - da toot. He blows it eight to the bar ___ in "boo-gie" rhy - thm. He
C
G
can't blow a note un - less a bass and gui - tar ___ is play - in' with him. ___
D7
C7
He makes the comp-'ny jump when he plays re - veil - le, He's the
G
1
2
Boo - gie Woo-gie Bu-gle Boy of Com-pa - ny B. ___ He Com-pa - ny B.

Lazy River
CHORDS USED IN THIS SONG:
Bb Bb7 Bdim C7 C13 C9 Cm7 Cm9 Db9 Dm7b5 Eb Edim
F7 F9 Gb9 G7 Ab7 A7
Words and Music by
HOAGY CARMICHAEL & SIDNEY ARODIN
Moderato
mf
Up a la - zy ri - ver by the old mill - run, That la - zy, la - zy ri - ver in the
noon - day sun, Lin - ger in the shade of a kind old tree,
Throw a-way your trou - bles, dream a dream with me.
Up a La - zy Ri - ver where the
ro - bin's song, A - wakes a bright new morn - ing, we can loaf a - long.
Blue skies up a - bove, ev' - ry one's in love, Up a La - zy Ri - ver, how
hap - py you can be, Up a La - zy Ri - ver with me.
me.

Big Noise from Winnetka

CHORDS USED IN THIS SONG:

Am6 Bm7♭5 E7♭9 E7 F7

Lyric by
GIL RODIN & BOB CROSBY

Music by
BOB HAGGART & RAY BAUDUC

Night Train

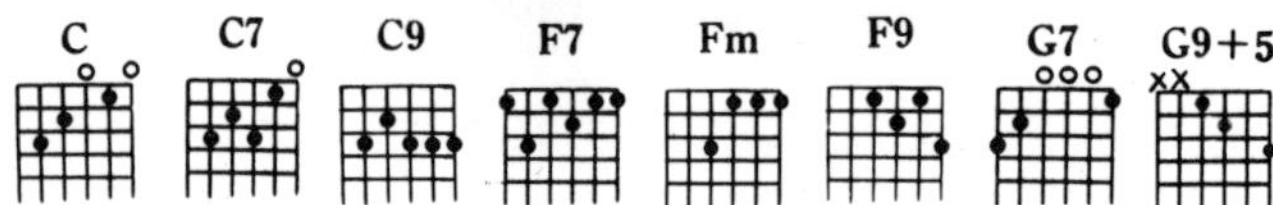

Words by
OSCAR WASHINGTON & LEWIS C. SIMPKINS

Music by
JIMMY FOREST

Swing blues

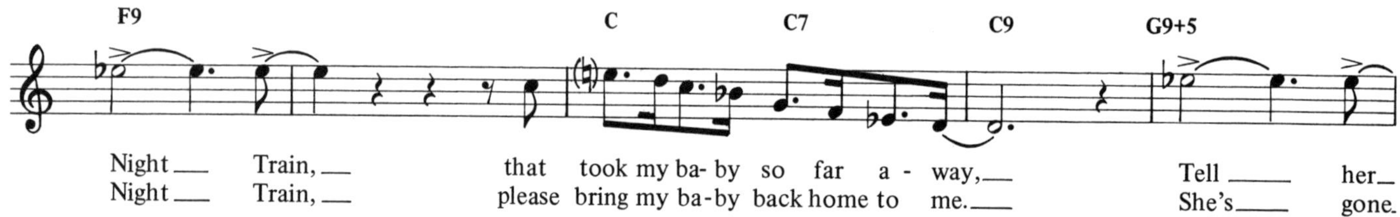

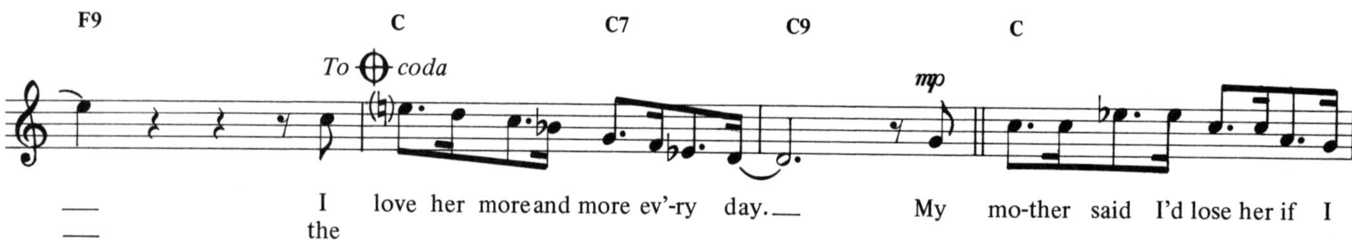

C C
f mf
ba - by was a bless - in', should have list-ened. Night__ Train,__ your
C7 C9 F9
whis - tle tore my poor heart in two,__ Night ____ Train,__ your
C C7 C9 G9+5 F9
whis - tle tore my poor heart in two,__ She's ____ gone,__ and
C C7 C9 C Fm
mp
I don't know what I'm gon-na do.__ It's blue Mon - day morn-ing,____ She left me
C7 F7
last ____ Sat-ur - day night, Now it's blue Mon - day morn - ing,____ She left me
C7 F7
last ____ Sat - ur - day night, Ev' - ry time I hear trains blow____ I get the
C C7 C
D.S. al Coda
blues,__Can't sleep at night.
CODA
C G7 C C9
rall.
f p
blues she left just won't set me free.

Nobody's Sweetheart

CHORDS USED IN THIS SONG:

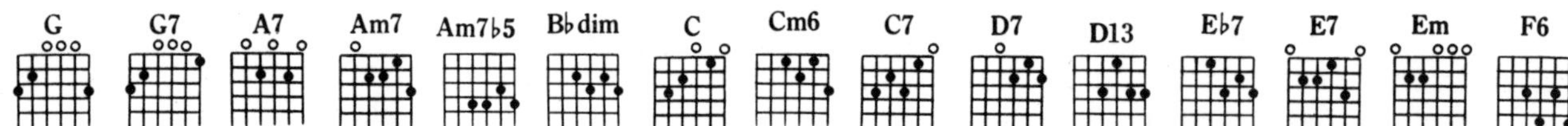

Words and Music by
GUS KAHN, ERNIE ERDMAN, BILLY MEYERS & ELMER SCHOEBEL

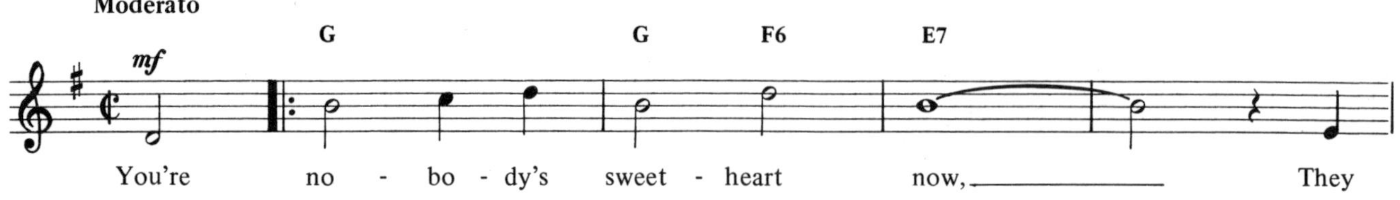

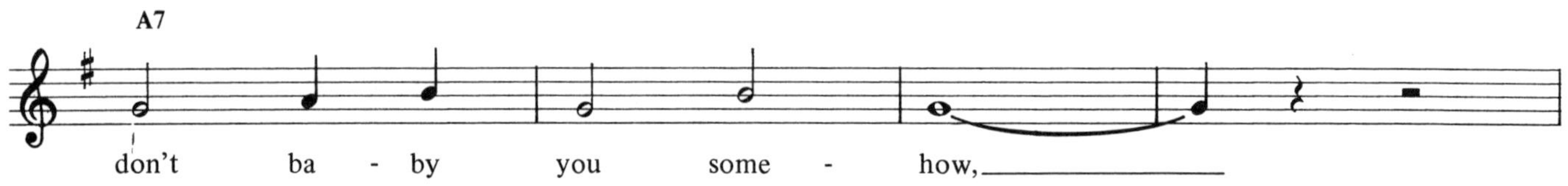

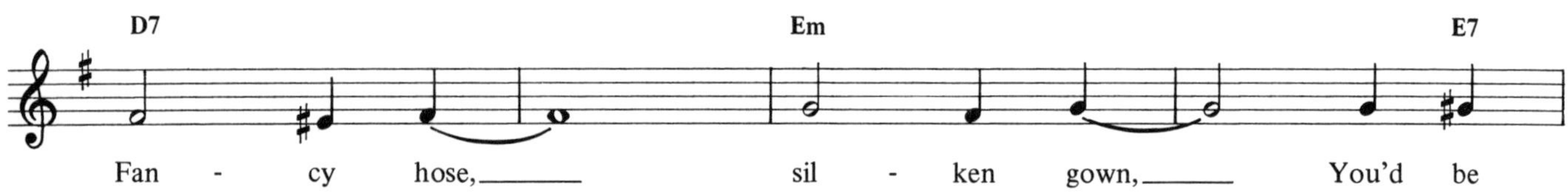

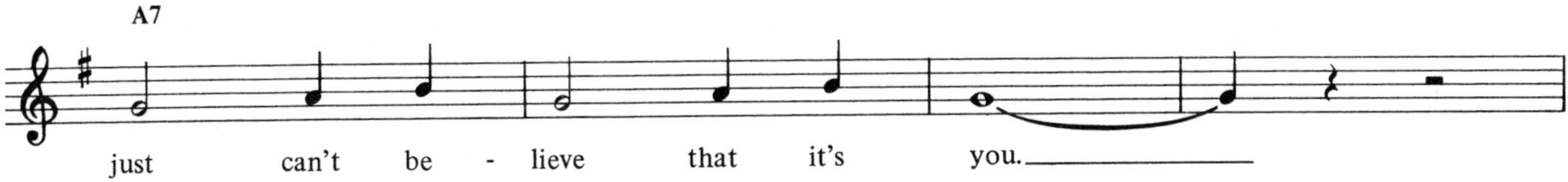
A7
just can't be - lieve that it's you.

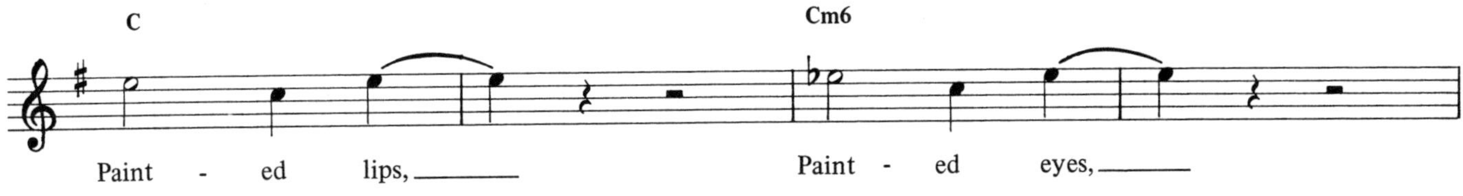
C
Cm6
Paint - ed lips,
Paint - ed eyes,

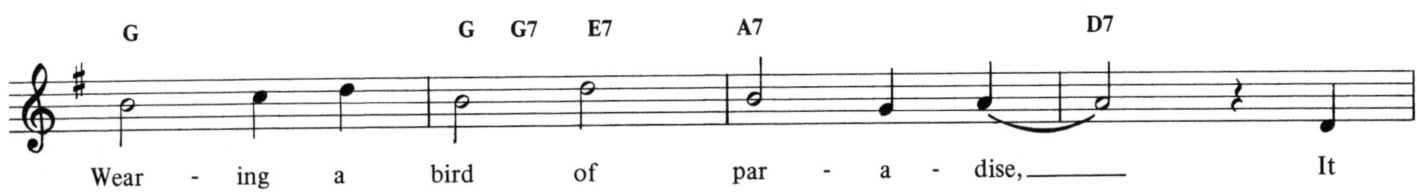
G
G G7 E7
A7
D7
Wear - ing a bird of par - a - dise,
It

G
G F6
E7
Am7 Am7♭5
all seems wrong some - how,
That you're no - bo - dy's

1
2
D13 D7
G B♭dim
Am7
D7
G C7
G
sweet - heart now.
You're now.

Take Five

CHORDS USED IN THIS COMPOSITION:
Dm Dm7 F Fmaj7 Gm Gm7 Am7 A7 B♭ C7
by
PAUL DESMOND
mp
(sim.)
mf
D.S. al coda
CODA
p

Organ Grinder's Swing

CHORDS USED IN THIS SONG:

G
C7
C6
D7

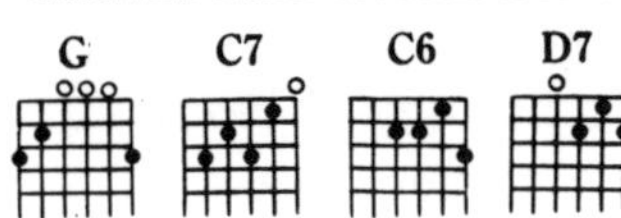

Words by
MITCHELL PARISH & IRVIN MILLS

Music by
WILL HUDSON

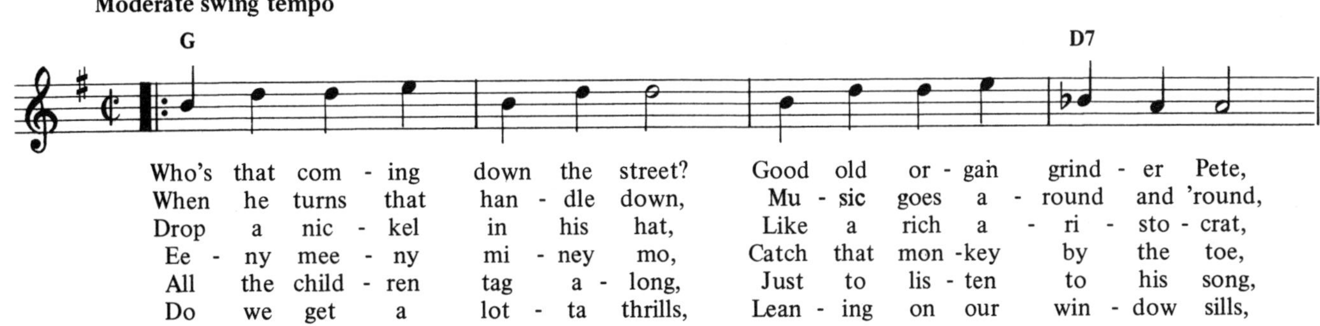

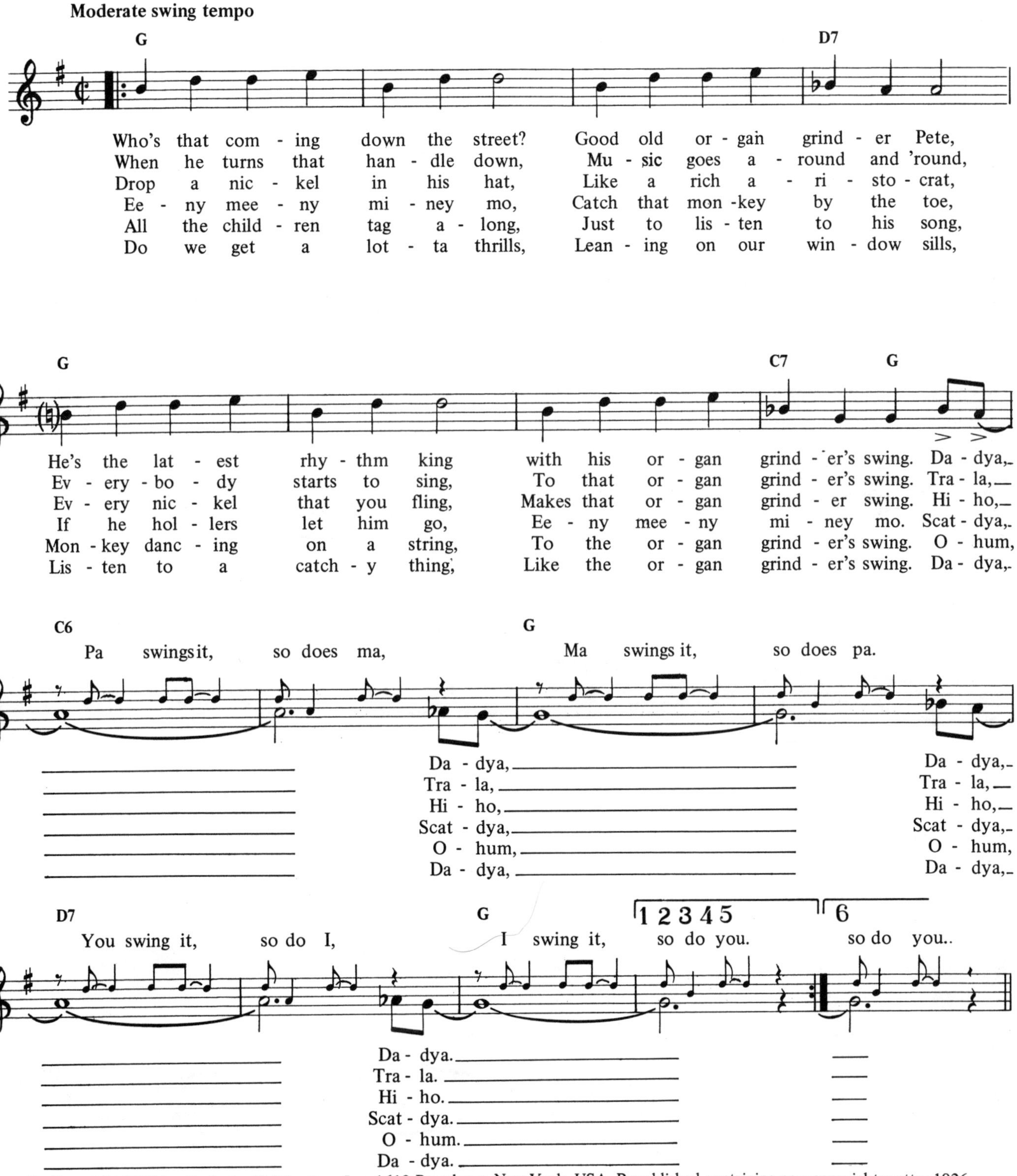

Moderate swing tempo
G
D7
Who's that com - ing down the street? Good old or - gan grind - er Pete,
When he turns that han - dle down, Mu - sic goes a - round and 'round,
Drop a nic - kel in his hat, Like a rich a - ri - sto - crat,
Ee - ny mee - ny mi - ney mo, Catch that mon - key by the toe,
All the child - ren tag a - long, Just to lis - ten to his song,
Do we get a lot - ta thrills, Lean - ing on our win - dow sills,
G
C7
G
He's the lat - est rhy - thm king with his or - gan grind - er's swing. Da - dya,
Ev - ery - bo - dy starts to sing, To that or - gan grind - er's swing. Tra - la,
Ev - ery nic - kel that you fling, Makes that or - gan grind - er swing. Hi - ho,
If he hol - lers let him go, Ee - ny mee - ny mi - ney mo. Scat - dya,
Mon - key danc - ing on a string, To the or - gan grind - er's swing. O - hum,
Lis - ten to a catch - y thing, Like the or - gan grind - er's swing. Da - dya,
C6
G
Pa swings it, so does ma, Ma swings it, so does pa.
Da - dya, Da - dya,
Tra - la, Tra - la,
Hi - ho, Hi - ho,
Scat - dya, Scat - dya,
O - hum, O - hum,
Da - dya, Da - dya,
D7
G
1 2 3 4 5
6
You swing it, so do I, I swing it, so do you. so do you..
Da - dya.
Tra - la.
Hi - ho.
Scat - dya.
O - hum.
Da - dya.

It's A Raggy Waltz

G6
G7
C7
Gdim
G6
E7♭9
A7♭9
D7
G6
D11
G6
C6
Bm7
B♭m7
E♭7
A♭6
Gm7
Fm6
Am7
Am7♭5
D7
G
Am7
Gdim
G6
G7
C7
Gdim
G6
E7♭9
A7♭9
D7♭9
G6
D11
G6
G6
C9
Am7
D7
G6

It Don't Mean A Thing (If It Ain't Got That Swing)

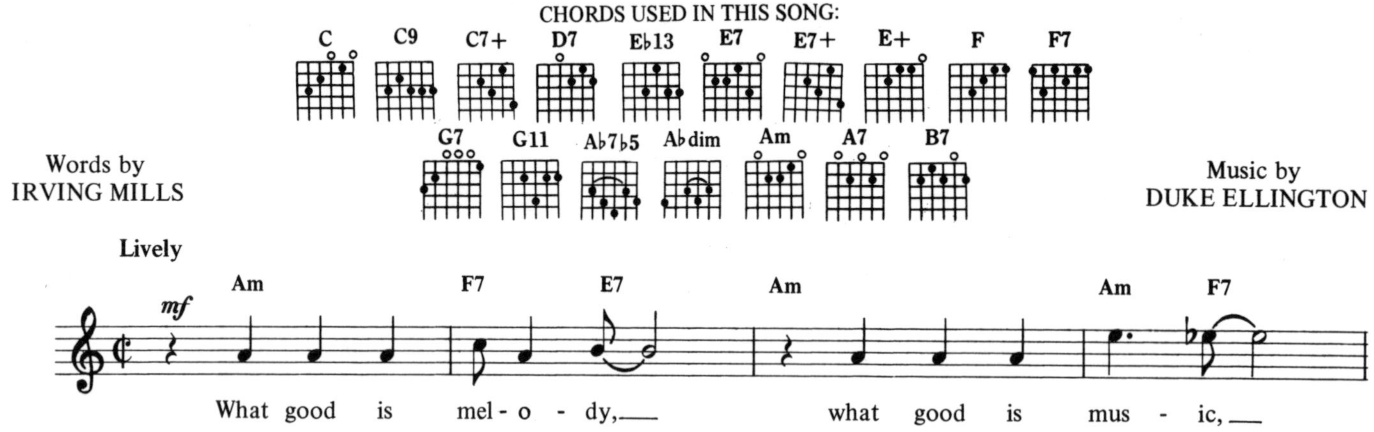

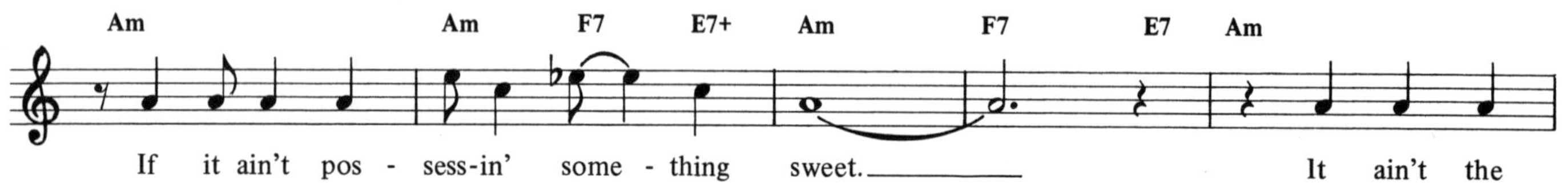

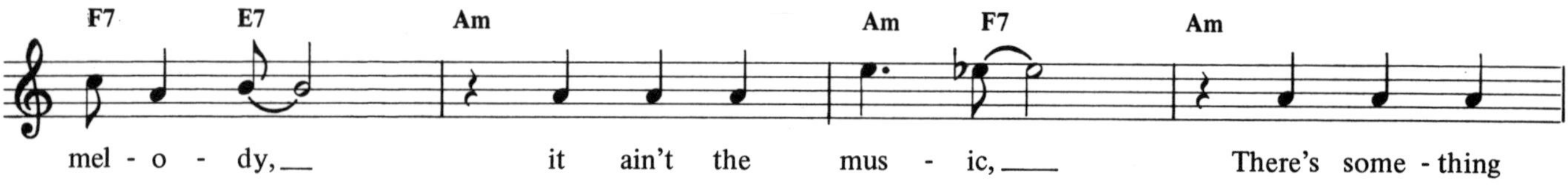

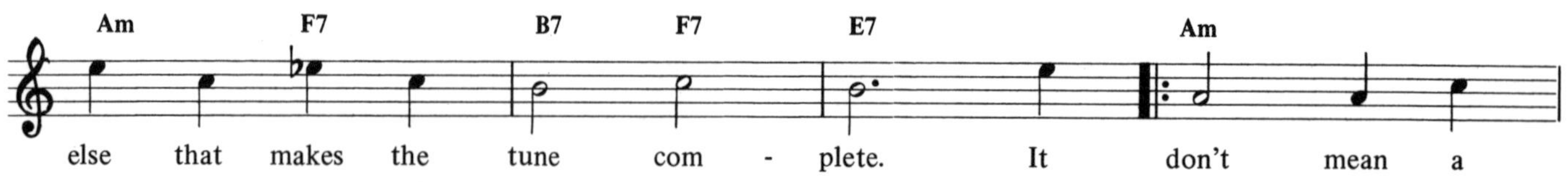

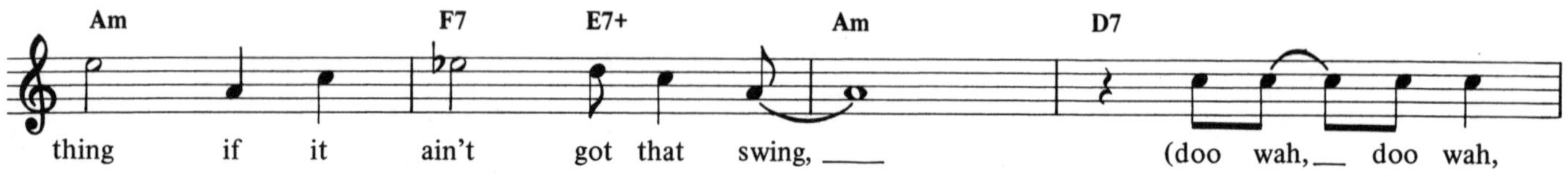

Ab7b5 G11 C E+ Am
doo wah, doo wah, doo wah, doo wah, doo wah, doo wah) It don't mean a

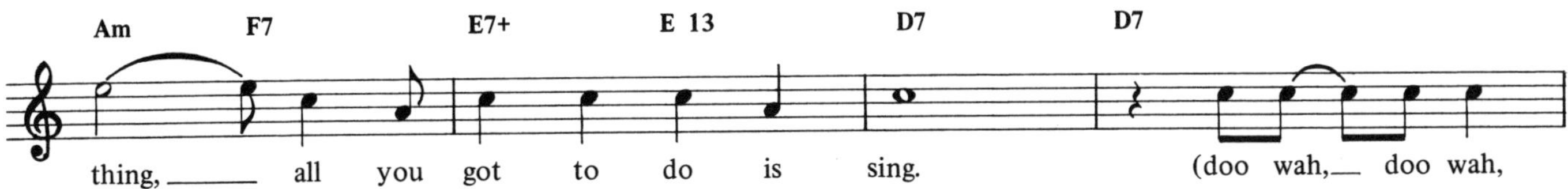
Am F7 E7+ E 13 D7 D7
thing, all you got to do is sing. (doo wah, doo wah,

Ab7b5 G11 C C9
doo wah, doo wah, doo wah, doo wah, doo wah, doo wah.) It makes no diff'rence if

C7+ F F D7 Abdim
it's sweet or hot, Just give that rhy - thm

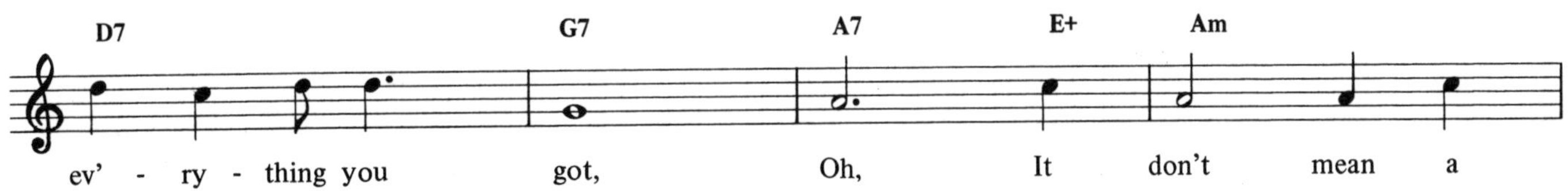
D7 G7 A7 E+ Am
ev' - ry - thing you got, Oh, It don't mean a

Am F7 E7+ Am D7
thing if it ain't got that swing, (doo wah, doo wah,

1 2
Ab7b5 G11 C E+ C
doo wah, doo wah, doo wah, doo wah, doo wah, doo wah.) It wah.)

Moanin'

CHORDS USED IN THIS SONG:
Am Am7 A7 A B7♭9 B♭ C7 D D9
D7♭9 D7 E7 Em7 E Fmaj7
Words by
JON HENDRICKS
Music by
BOBBY TIMMONS
Fairly slow
mf
Ev' - ry morn - in' finds me moan - in', 'cause of all the trou - ble I see,
Life's a los - in' gam - ble to me, cares and woes have got me moan - in',
ev' - ry eve - nin' finds me moan - in', I'm a - lone and cry - in' the blues.
I'm so tired of pay - in' these dues, Ev' - ry - bo - dy knows I'm moan - in'.
Lord I spend plen - ty of days and nights a - lone with my grief,
And I pray real - ly and tru - ly pray some - bo - dy will come and bring me re - lief.
Ev' - ry morn - in' finds me moan - in', 'cause of all the trou - bles I see,
Life's a los - in' gam - ble to me, cares and woes have got me moan - in',
Ev' - ry morn - in' finds me
ritard
p

Struttin' With Some Barbecue
CHORDS USED IN THIS SONG:
D6 D7 Dmaj7 E♭dim Em7 E7 Fm7 G6 G7 A♭dim A+ A7 B♭9 B+ Bm7 B9
Words by
DON RAYE
Music by
LOUIS ARMSTRONG
Tempo di strut
mf
Struttin' with some Bar - be - cue, Swing-in' with the band; Like the happy
peo - ple do, Way down in Dix-ie land. Hear that old trom - bone,
and the trum-pet ad lib, Love to hear the lick, while I do my
pick - in', Pick - in' on a juic - y rib I'm Strut-tin' with some Bar - be - cue,
Feel - ing might-y grand, Pass an - oth - er help - in' please,
Of that good old Dix - ie land, And Mis - ter Wai - ter if you please,
An - oth - er rib or two, And I'll go strut, strut, strut-tin' Strut-
tin' with some Bar-be - cue. Struttin' with some

Petite Fleur
(Little Flower)

by
SIDNEY BECHET

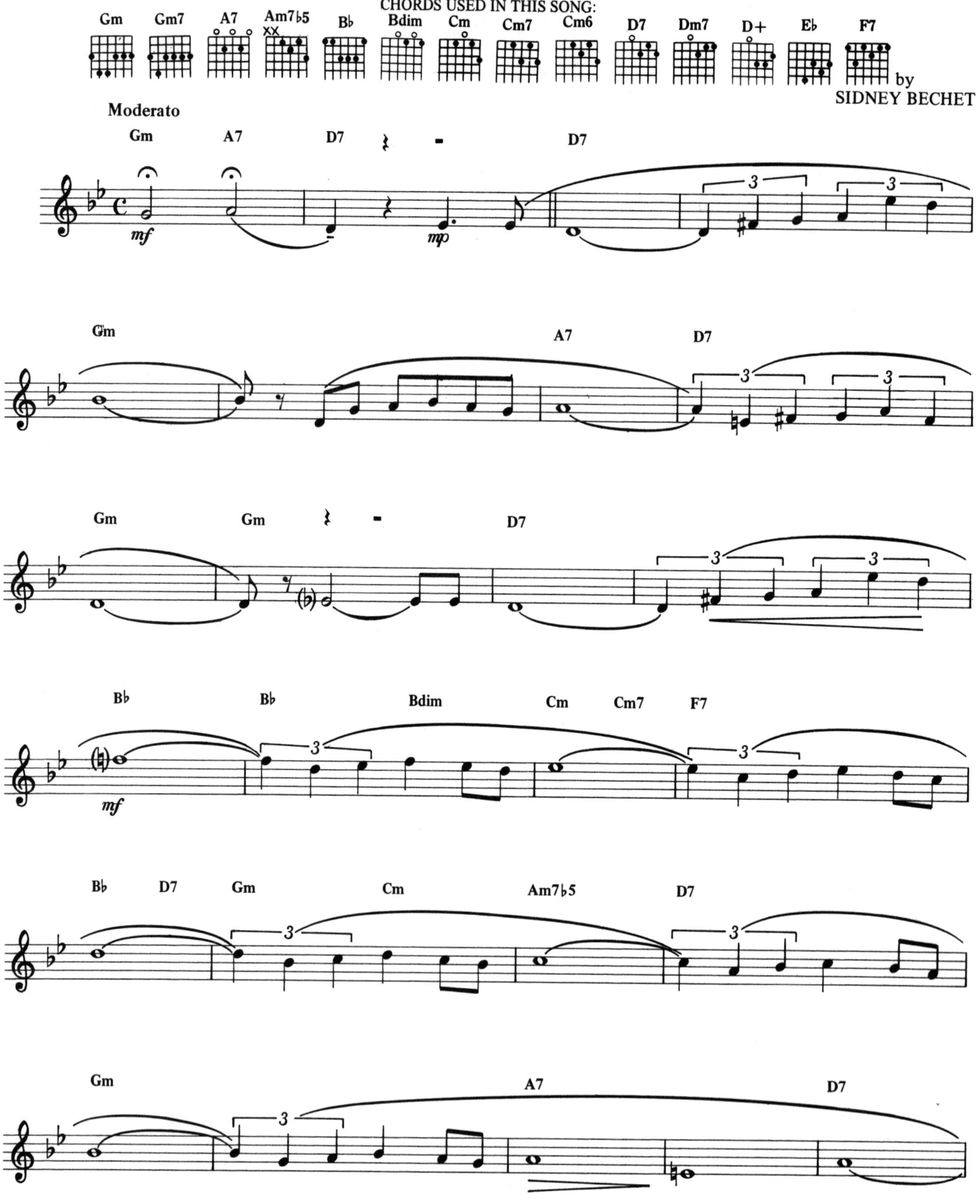

D7
D7
Gm
mp
Am7♭5
D+
D7
Gm
Cm
Gm
G7
G7
Dm7
G7
Cm
mf
Cm6
Cm
Cm6
F7
B♭
E♭
D7
D7
Gm
mp
Am7♭5
D+
D7
Gm
Cm
Gm

Lullaby Of Birdland

CHORDS USED IN THIS SONG:

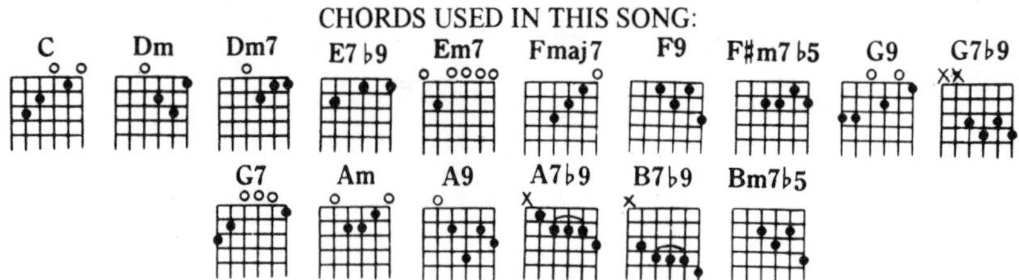

Words by
GEORGE DAVID WEISS

Music by
GEORGE SHEARING

Moderato

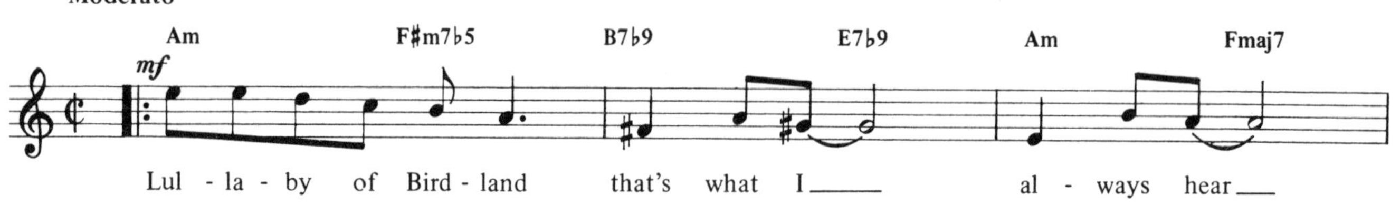

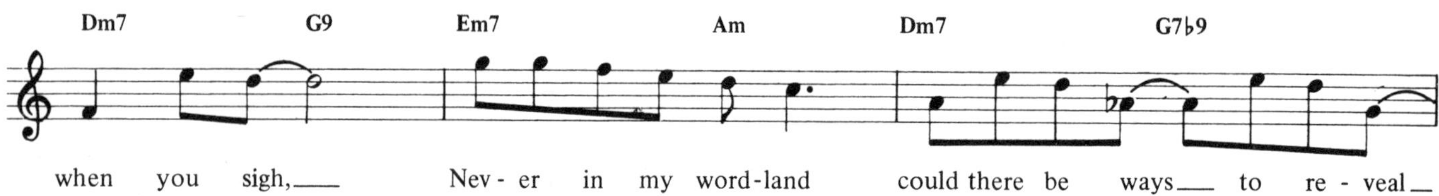

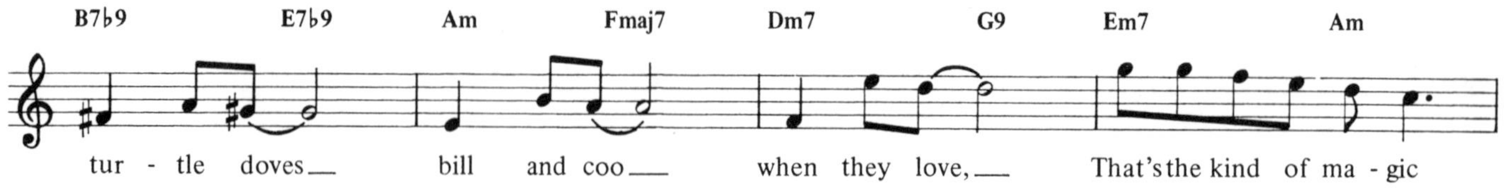

Dm G9 G7♭9 C A9 A7♭9
- low, He real - ly knows how to cry! That's how I'd cry in my pil -

Dm G9 G7♭9 C E7
- low, If you should tell me fare - well and good - bye!

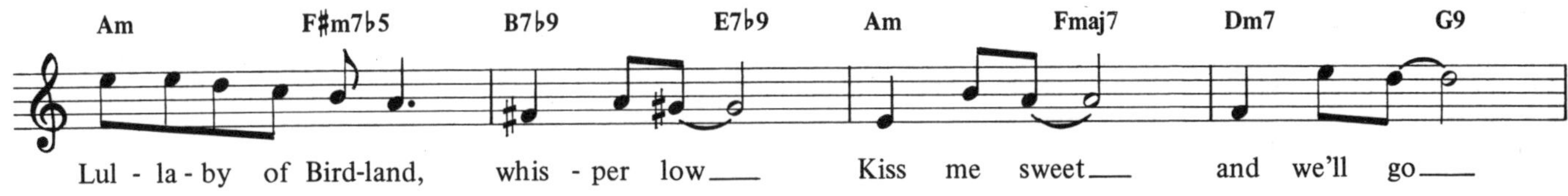
Am F♯m7♭5 B7♭9 E7♭9 Am Fmaj7 Dm7 G9
Lul - la - by of Bird-land, whis - per low Kiss me sweet and we'll go

1
Em7 Am Dm G7♭9 C F9 Bm7♭5 E7
fly - in' high in Bird-land High in the sky up a - bove all be - cause we're in love!

2
C Dm7 G9 G7♭9 C F9 C
all be - cause we're in love!

Moonglow

Words and Music by
WILL HUDSON, EDDIE DeLANGE & IRVING MILLS

Way Down Yonder In New Orleans

When The Saints Go Marching In

CHORDS USED IN THIS SONG:

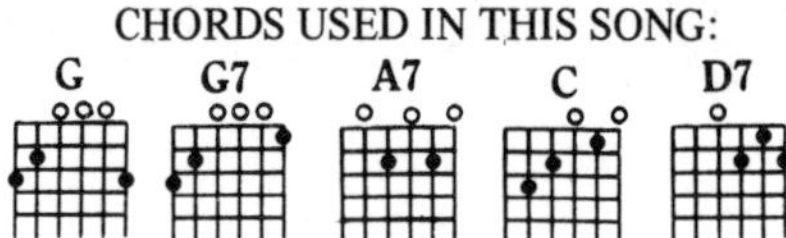

Traditional

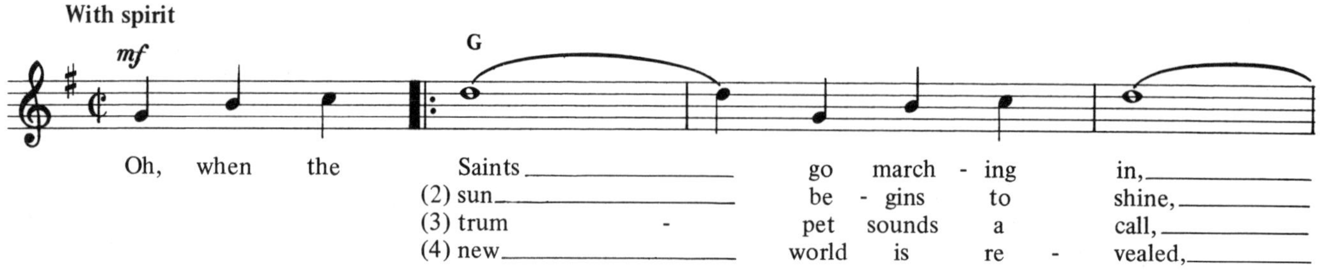

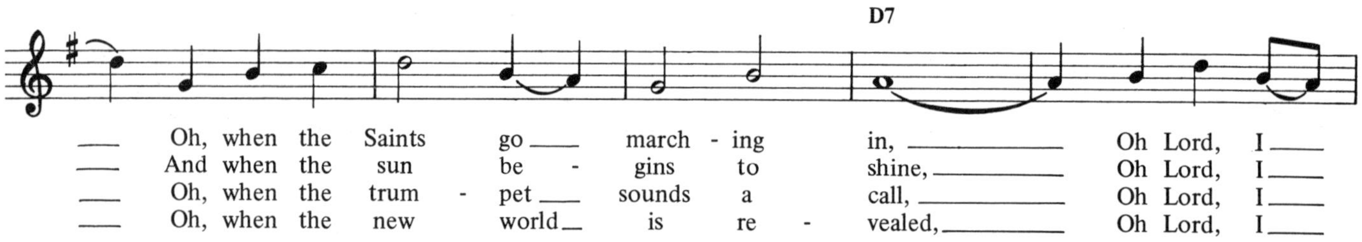

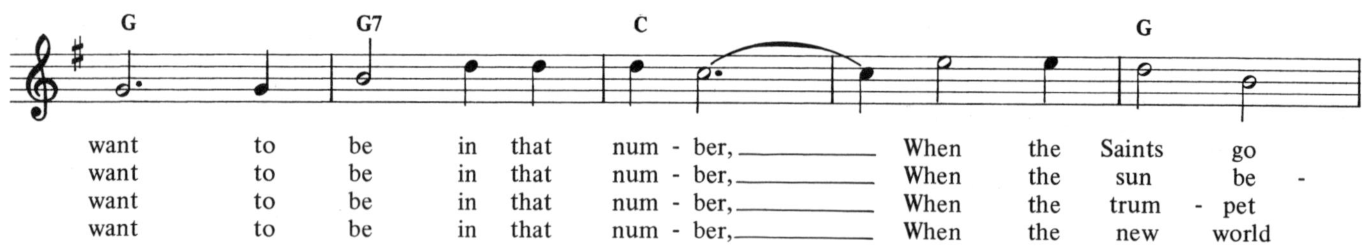

The Swingin' Shepherd Blues

CHORDS USED IN THIS SONG:

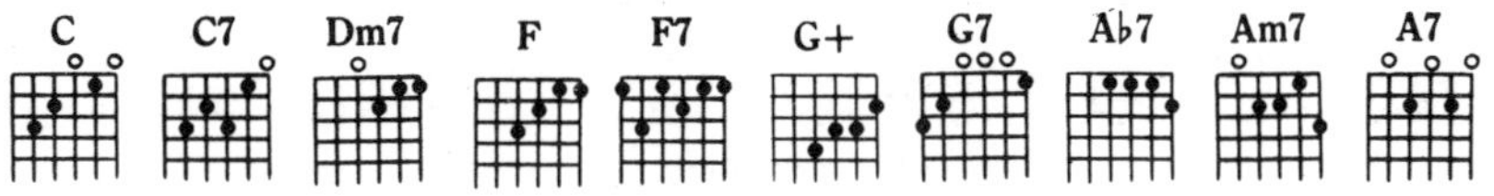

C C7 Dm7 F F7 G+ G7 A♭7 Am7 A7

Words by
RHODA ROBERTS & KENNY JACOBSON

Music by
MOE KOFFMAN

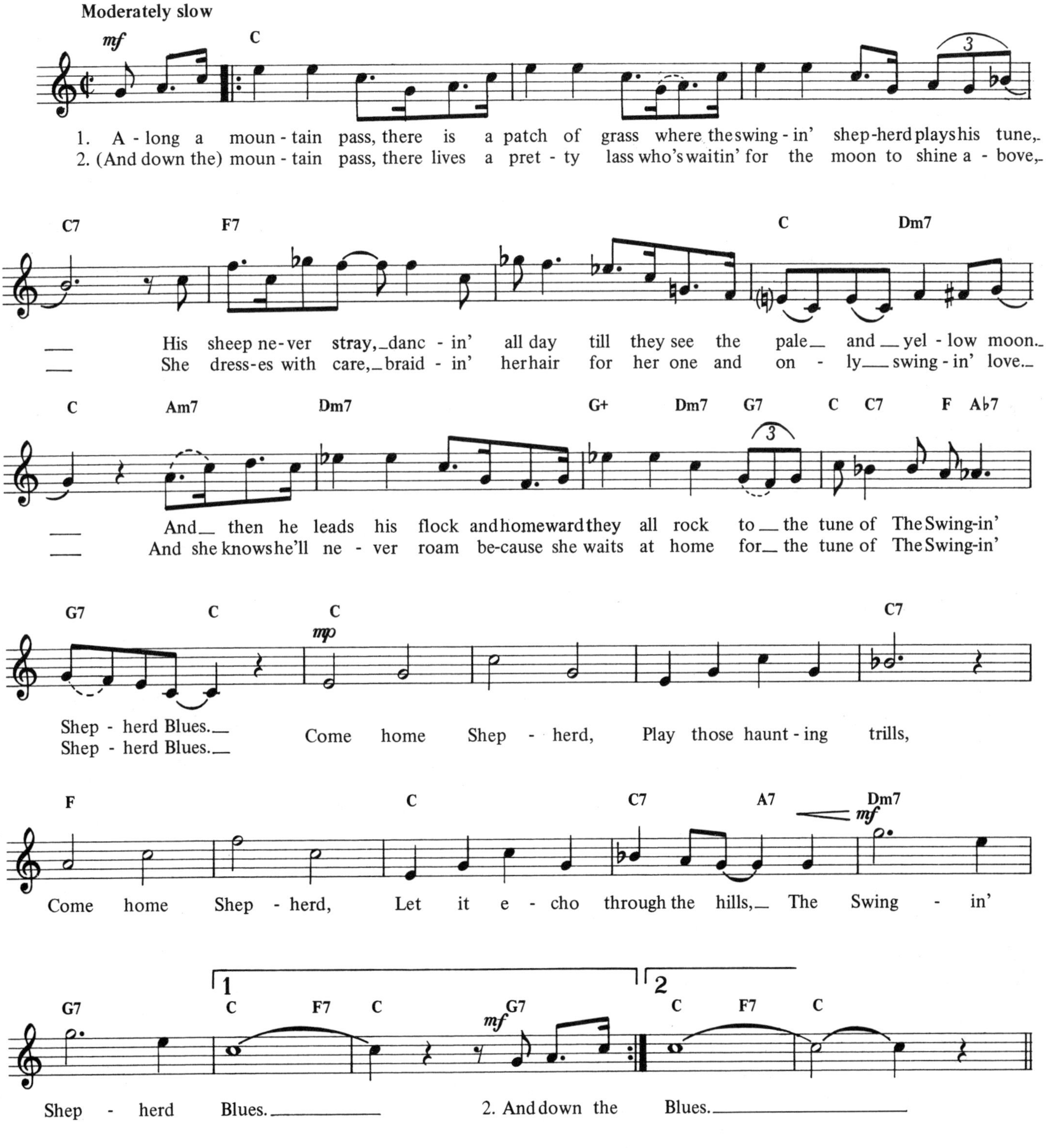

Moderately slow

1. A - long a moun - tain pass, there is a patch of grass where the swing - in' shep - herd plays his tune,
2. (And down the) moun - tain pass, there lives a pret - ty lass who's waitin' for the moon to shine a - bove,

C7 F7 C Dm7

His sheep ne - ver stray, danc - in' all day till they see the pale and yel - low moon.
She dress - es with care, braid - in' her hair for her one and on - ly swing - in' love.

C Am7 Dm7 G+ Dm7 G7 C C7 F A♭7

And then he leads his flock and homeward they all rock to the tune of The Swing - in'
And she knows he'll ne - ver roam be - cause she waits at home for the tune of The Swing - in'

G7 C C mp C7

Shep - herd Blues.
Shep - herd Blues.
Come home Shep - herd, Play those haunt - ing trills,

F C C7 A7 mf Dm7

Come home Shep - herd, Let it e - cho through the hills, The Swing - in'

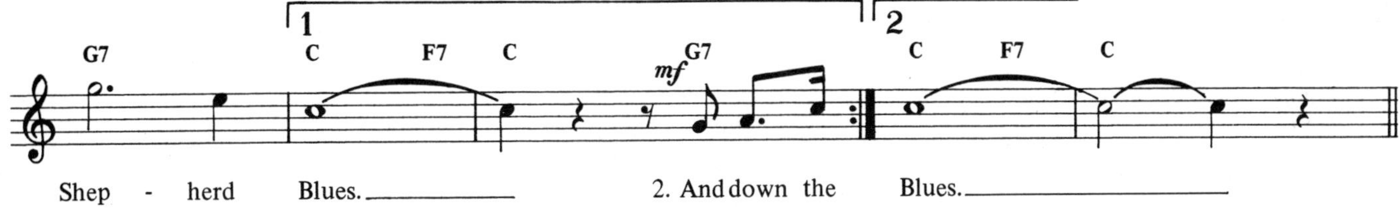

Farewell Blues